Congressional
Research
Service

Offsets, Supplemental Appropriations, and the Disaster Relief Fund: FY1990-FY2013

William L. Painter
Analyst in Emergency Management and Homeland Security Policy

December 4, 2012

Congressional Research Service

7-5700

www.crs.gov

R42458

CRS Report for Congress —————————————————

Prepared for Members and Committees of Congress

Summary

This report discusses the recent history of offsetting rescissions in paying for supplemental appropriations to the Federal Emergency Management Agency's Disaster Relief Fund (DRF).

As Congress has debated the growing size of the budget deficit and national debt in recent years, efforts have intensified to control spending and offset the costs of legislation. In 1995, 2011, and again in 2012, the question of offsetting disaster relief spending emerged in congressional debate. In 2011, a series of disasters threatened to deplete the DRF, which is the primary source of assistance to state and local governments as well as individuals in the wake of disasters.

Hurricane Sandy struck the east coast of the United States on October 29, 2012. The storm caused tens of billions of dollars in damage along the coast. As damage estimates became public in the weeks after the storm, calls for supplemental appropriations to help pay for recovery efforts were met with calls for offsets from some quarters.

Traditionally, supplemental disaster relief funding has been treated as emergency spending, not counted against discretionary budget caps, and not requiring an offset. However, supplemental spending packages have at times carried rescissions that have offset, to one degree or another, their budgetary impact. In some instances, the supplemental spending packages have contained both appropriations for the DRF and offsetting rescissions.

This report examines the use of offsets in connection with supplemental funding for the DRF since FY1990, reviewing three specific incidences where bills that had an impact on the level of funding available in the DRF were fully offset, and points out a number of issues Congress may wish to consider in this debate.

Since FY1990, there has only been one case in which supplemental funding for the DRF was completely offset by rescissions.

This report will be updated as events warrant.

Contents

Figures

Tables

Appendixes

Contacts

Overview

One longstanding policy question facing Congress is how to budget for and deal with the unexpected costs incurred in emergency response.

Before Hurricane Sandy, this question had most recently entered the debate in FY2011 as part of larger discussions about how government funding decisions impact the economy, the budget deficit, and the national debt. In May 2011, the House Appropriations Committee proposed offsetting a billion dollars of emergency supplemental appropriations for the Federal Emergency Management Agency's (FEMA's) Disaster Relief Fund—the primary source of federal government assistance for people and communities affected by major disasters—which was depleted at a faster rate than had been projected due to a number of major storms and floods earlier in the year. The House rescinded unspent money from another department's budget to pay for the additional funding, in a proposal that was ultimately not supported in the Senate's version of the bill.

The Budget Control Act (P.L. 112-25), passed in the first session of the 112th Congress as part of a deal to raise the debt limit, literally changed the terms of the debate. The new law included provisions that outlined separate treatment for disaster relief, distinct from emergency funding. Furthermore, P.L. 112-25 redefined "disaster relief" as being federal government assistance provided pursuant to a major disaster declared under the Stafford Act, rather than assistance provided through the Disaster Relief Fund (DRF). Funding designated as disaster relief in future spending bills could be "paid for" by adjusting upward the discretionary spending caps. This allowable adjustment for disaster relief is limited, however, to an amount based on the ten-year rolling average of what has been spent by the federal government on relief efforts for major disasters.

Before these provisions could take effect, however, the issue of offsets for supplemental appropriations for the DRF returned to the debate as the House and Senate worked on stopgap funding legislation as FY2011 year drew to a close. The Department of Homeland Security's congressional authorizing committees also debated whether disaster assistance funding should be offset as they marked up their bills. No resolution was reached on the issue, as the fiscal year ended and the DRF was replenished through a continuing resolution.

The anticipated need for federal support for Hurricane Sandy relief is projected to exceed the available balance in the DRF for FY2013. Beginning in November 2012 there have been calls for supplemental appropriations for Hurricane Sandy relief efforts, as well as calls for offsets to pay for them.

These are recent occurrences, but the debate over offsetting emergency disaster funding is not entirely new. The result of congressional deliberations over the years has been that while disaster assistance from other agencies has at times been funded through shifting resources from one program to another through appropriations legislation, the DRF has generally been given a priority status and been funded promptly in times of need, without offsets.

This report outlines CRS's analysis of supplemental appropriations laws going back to 1990. We examined legislation with offsetting rescissions and provisions affecting the DRF, looking for connections between supplemental DRF funding and offsets. The analysis takes a detailed look at three cases where legislation affecting the DRF was fully offset, but ultimately finds that since

FY1990 Congress fully offset supplemental funding for the DRF through cuts elsewhere in the budget only once.

Definitions

Offsets

In the context of appropriations debate, to "offset" is to use policy changes, additional revenue, spending cuts, or rescissions of previous appropriations to "pay for" all or part of the cost of a piece of legislation. The final arbiter of the cost of a piece of legislation and the value of any offsets is the Congressional Budget Office, which provides budgetary "scoring" for legislation. Legislation that is "fully offset" has no overall net cost in budget authority or outlays. When a bill is partially offset, it can be difficult to associate a given offset with the specific appropriation it is intended to pay for.

One rare example of an overt linkage is in Title VI of the House-reported version of H.R. 2017, the FY2012 Homeland Security Appropriations bill. The provision reads as follows:

> Sec. 601. Effective on the date of the enactment of this Act, of the unobligated balances remaining available to the Department of Energy pursuant to section 129 of the Continuing Appropriations Resolution, 2009 (division A of P.L. 110-329), $500,000,000 is rescinded and $1,000,000,000 is hereby transferred to and merged with `Department of Homeland Security—Federal Emergency Management Agency—Disaster Relief`: *Provided*, That the amount transferred by this section is designated as an emergency pursuant to section 3(c)(1) of H.Res. 5 (112th Congress).

This section was added as a single amendment in full committee markup of the legislation, and provides a billion dollars of additional resources to the DRF, paying for it by transferring some resources and rescinding others.[1]

Offsetting provisions are not typically linked to other items in appropriations bills, but links may be identified through analysis of report language, other committee documents, or debate. For example, in S.Rept. 112-74, which accompanied the Senate's version of the FY2012 Homeland Security appropriations bill, the Senate recommended $18.3 million to replace damaged Coast Guard helicopters. The Senate bill also includes three rescissions totaling $18.3 million to offset that cost. As the rescission and funding are both carried in Section 565 of the bill, it is clear that the three rescissions offset the specific additional appropriation. If, however, the aircraft replacement funding was carried in the Coast Guard portion of Title II of the bill, rather than in Title V in the same section as the rescissions, one might not link the rescissions to the additional funding; as there were more than $103 million of other rescissions that simply lowered the budgetary score of the bill and were not directly associated with any other appropriations provisions.[2]

---

[1] The $500,000,000 in rescissions is needed to compensate for the lower projected rate of spending from the original account. For a more in-depth discussion of procedural considerations for offsetting amendments, see CRS Report RL31055, *House Offset Amendments to Appropriations Bills: Procedural Considerations*, by Jessica Tollestrup.

[2] In this case, the funding and rescissions represent the full extent of emergency funding in the bill, which would provide an extra piece of evidence, but the illustration remains valid.

Supplemental Appropriations

Supplemental appropriations are budget authority provided by Congress over and above the budget authority in the annual appropriations bills. Supplemental appropriations can be made through stand-alone supplemental appropriations legislation, or as part of a general appropriations bill.[3]

Disaster Relief v. Disaster Assistance

The terms "disaster relief" and "disaster assistance" are often used interchangeably to describe support provided to communities in the wake of a disaster. For the purposes of this discussion, "disaster relief" refers to resources provided through the Federal Emergency Management Agency (FEMA) Disaster Relief Fund (DRF).[4] "Disaster assistance" is a broader category which includes other assistance funding for disaster-struck communities. These funds are managed not only through FEMA, but through many other federal agencies and departments. The core analysis of this report deals with supplemental disaster relief, rather than the broader disaster assistance category.

Offsetting Supplemental Disaster Relief

According to the most recent CBO analysis, FEMA has been the second-largest recipient of supplemental appropriations, behind only the Department of Defense.[5] Most of these appropriations have been for disaster relief.

From January 1, 1990, to November 31, 2012, there have been 59 bills signed into law that included supplemental appropriations.

As **Figure 1** indicates, thirty-one of these have included rescissions to offset some of the discretionary budget authority in the legislation—an analysis of these bills identified eighteen that carried provisions affecting the DRF. None had provisions explicitly linking their rescissions to additional monies for the DRF. However, six of the bills with rescissions had spending reductions of such a size that the entire cost of the bill was offset.[6] Three of those fully offset bills carried provisions affecting the DRF. These bills merited a closer examination to see whether these were

---

[3] For additional discussion of the history of supplemental appropriations bills and their budgetary impacts, see CRS Report RL33134, *Supplemental Appropriations: Trends and Budgetary Impacts Since 1981*, by Thomas L. Hungerford.

[4] It is important to note that this definition differs from the definition of "disaster relief" under the Budget Control Act (BCA, P.L. 112-25). The BCA defines disaster relief as federal funding provided pursuant to a major disaster declaration under the Stafford Act. As required by the BCA, the Office of Management and Budget made a calculation of which funding met that definition for the FY2001-FY2010 in September 2011. Their calculation reached well beyond the activities of the DRF and FEMA, but does not reach years prior to 2001, and cannot be replicated for those years at this time. Therefore, for the sake of consistency, this report does not use the BCA definition in its analysis.

[5] Ellen Hayes, *Supplemental Appropriations in the 1990s*, Congressional Budget Office, Washington, DC, March 2001, http://www.cbo.gov.

[6] Congressional Budget Office, *History of Supplemental Appropriations*, CBO Data on Supplemental Budget Authority from 2000 to 2010, and *Supplemental Appropriations in the 1990s*, Washington, DC, http://www.cbo.gov.

---

cases where supplemental disaster relief was paid for by offsetting cuts to other parts of the budget.[7]

Figure 1. Supplemental Appropriations, Rescissions, and Disaster Relief

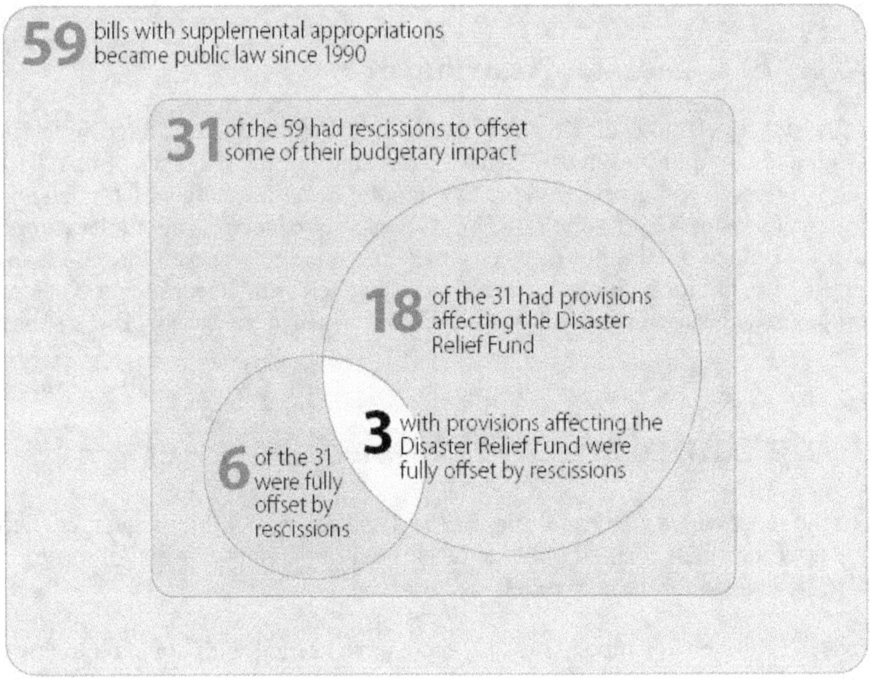

Source: CRS analysis of CBO data and legislative text.

Notes: Not to scale. Data current as of November 31, 2012.

The background on each of these three instances follows. As these analyses illustrate, supplemental disaster relief has only been fully offset once since 1990.

Emergency Supplemental and Rescissions for Antiterrorism and Oklahoma City Disaster, 1995 (P.L. 104-19)

Shortly after taking control of the U.S. Senate and House of Representatives in the 1994 midterm elections, the new Republican majority began to assemble a large rescissions package to cut previously approved spending for FY1995. The Clinton Administration submitted a package of rescissions and supplemental spending for FY1995 with their FY1996 budget legislation—a package that included $2.2 billion in rescissions and $10.4 billion in additional spending. The requested additional spending included $6.7 billion in funding for the DRF.[8] Speaker Newt

---

[7] **Table A-1** in the Appendix provides a list of bills including supplemental appropriations and offsetting rescissions from FY1990 to FY2012.

[8] President's Budget Request for FY1996, Budget Appendix, Supplemental Proposals, p. 1095.

Gingrich wrote a letter to the White House, asking for offsets for the additional spending.[9] Testifying before the House Appropriations Committee, Alice Rivlin, Director of the Office of Management and Budget at the time, declined to provide additional offsets, saying: "We believe our supplemental request should be treated as an emergency and not require offsets."

> We believe that the law established the authority for the President and the Congress to exempt genuine emergencies from the statutory caps, and the emergencies in question, which include the Northridge earthquake, are exactly the kinds of emergencies for which the authority was created.
>
> The Bush administration used the authority. This Administration has used the authority, with the concurrence of the Congress, for several emergencies over the past few years, including the Midwest floods, hurricanes, and other acts of God.
>
> So we believe that our supplemental request for additional spending on recovery from these emergencies should be treated as an emergency and should not require offsets.[10]

The House Appropriations Committee proposed cutting more than $17 billion in FY1995 spending while providing $5.4 billion for the DRF.[11] The Senate Appropriations Committee developed a smaller $13.5 billion spending package, which funded the Administration's full $6.7 billion request for the DRF.[12]

While the bill was before the conference committee, an additional request from the Administration for $142 million in assistance related to the Oklahoma City bombing came to the Congress. The initial conference agreement included $16.4 billion in rescissions, $6.7 billion for the DRF, and an additional $251 million for needs stemming from the bombing.[13] Although both chambers passed the agreement, the President vetoed it largely in response to the makeup of the rescissions package. A new package was approved seven weeks after the original veto, containing $16.3 billion in rescissions, $6.6 billion for the DRF, and $290 million for needs stemming from the bombing (roughly half for Oklahoma City, one half for anti-terrorism measures).[14]

In this case, the Congressional majority clearly stated an intent to offset the Administration's supplemental budget requests, regardless of their emergency designation. Some Members criticized the creation of linkages between traditionally politically popular disaster assistance funding and more divisive spending reductions and tax legislation.[15]

---

[9] Alan Fram, "Clinton, Republicans Tangle Over Quake Aid," *Daily News [Los Angeles, CA]*, February 15, 1995, p. N8, Valley edition.

[10] U.S. Congress, House Committee on Appropriations, *Federal Budget for 1996*, 104th Cong., 1st sess., February 14, 1995 (Washington: GPO, 1995), p.73.

[11] U.S. Congress, House Committee on Appropriations, *Making Emergency Supplemental Appropriations for Additional Disaster Assistance and Making Rescissions for the Fiscal Year Ending September 30, 1995, and for Other Purposes*, report to accompany H.R. 1158, 104th Cong., 1st sess., March 8, 1995, H.Rept. 104-70 (Washington: GPO, 1995).

[12] Sen. Robert Byrd, "The Emergency Supplemental Appropriations Act," remarks in the Senate, *Congressional Record*, vol. 142, part 1 (March 29, 1995), p. S4762.

[13] Sen. Mark Hatfield and Sen. Robert Byrd, "Second Supplemental Appropriations and Rescission Act, 1995," remarks in the Senate, *Congressional Record*, vol. 142, part 1 (May 24, 1995), p. S7372.

[14] *Emergency Supplemental Appropriations for Additional Disaster Assistance, for Anti-terrorism Initiatives, for Assistance in the Recovery from the Tragedy that Occurred at Oklahoma City, and Rescissions Act, 1995*, P.L. 104-19.

[15] "Emergency Supplemental Appropriations for Additional Disaster Assistance and Rescissions for Fiscal Year 1995," (continued...)

Representative Anthony Beilenson, in the minority at the time, made these remarks in debate on the original House package: "Combining these two matters—emergency assistance and rescissions—into one piece of legislation leaves us with the unfair choice of voting either for emergency assistance and against adequate funding for a great many other programs we support, or against emergency assistance and for retaining existing funding for those other programs."[16] Speaking for the majority, the Chairman of the Appropriations Committee, Representative Robert Livingston claimed the bill set a historic precedent, calling it "the first time an emergency supplemental has ever been paid for in history,"[17] although the House had already passed an emergency supplemental appropriations bill for the Department of Defense in February 1995 that had been offset.[18]

It is important to note that the new Congressional majority had already announced their plan to bring forward a rescission package at the opening meeting of the House Appropriations Committee, where the Chairman famously illustrated his intent by displaying a collection of large knives. While the deficit-reduction agenda outlined by Chairman Livingston prior to the supplemental request may have been the original motive for the rescissions package, P.L. 104-19 is a clear case where supplemental appropriations for the DRF were directly and fully offset by cuts to other parts of the budget.

FY1996 Omnibus Consolidated Appropriations and Rescission Act (H.R. 2019, P.L. 104-134)

In February 1996, Congress was faced with resolving six appropriations bills in the wake of a budgetary standoff that had resulted in government shutdowns. That month, the Administration amended their budget request to provide additional resources for FY1996. H.R. 3019 would be the vehicle for the resolution of those six unfinished appropriations bills and the Administration's request for additional funds. The final conference agreement on those unfinished bills included $222 million for the base budget for the DRF,[19] but rescinded $1 billion from the contingent disaster relief funding (a type of emergency funding that is contingent upon a request from the administration) provided to the DRF just months earlier in P.L. 104-129.[20] This was the largest single offset to the funding provided in the bill.

It is worth noting that part of the debate on H.R. 3019 addressed offsets for disaster *assistance*, which is generally considered to be a broader category of disaster funding, going beyond what is provided through the DRF to encompass disaster aid provided through other components of the federal government. The original House version of the bill included offsets for disaster assistance. During Senate consideration of the bill, several amendments were offered and withdrawn that proposed offsets for disaster assistance funding. None of these were brought to a vote. However, the conference report notes that Senate provisions calling for offsets for disaster assistance were

---

(...continued)

House debate, *Congressional Record*, March 16, 1995, pgs. H.R. 3296.

[16] Ibid, p. H3296.

[17] Ibid, p. H3301.

[18] *Emergency Supplemental Appropriations and Rescissions for the Department of Defense to Preserve and Enhance Military Readiness Act of 1995*, P.L. 104-6.

[19] H.Rept. 104-537, p. 311.

[20] H.Rept. 104-537, p. 370.

dropped from the bill as unnecessary, as both the original House legislation and the conference agreement included adequate offsets for disaster assistance.[21]

While this legislation is an example of disaster assistance being offset, there are two primary reasons to exclude P.L. 104-134 as an example of supplemental appropriations for the DRF being offset. First, while the bill did include new budget authority for the DRF, this was not a supplemental—the new budget authority was the *regular* appropriation for the DRF for FY1996. Second, although the legislation is offset, the billion-dollar rescission taken from the DRF meant the DRF faced a net loss of $778 million from the legislation. Therefore, by not providing supplemental appropriations to the DRF and actually using DRF funds to pay for supplemental appropriations for other government elements, this legislation is not an example of supplemental funding for the DRF being offset.

Division B of the FY2006 Defense Appropriations Act (P.L. 109-148)

Hurricane Katrina struck the Gulf Coast on August 29, 2005. Ten days later, Congress had passed two laws that provided $60 billion in emergency funding to the DRF. Both measures were enacted one day after the requests were received.[22] Preliminary cost estimates varied widely and lacked a basis in facts, which were still in short supply, as flood waters had yet to recede, preventing damage assessments and cost estimates from being made.[23] After an initial spike in spending to meet emergency needs, as the recovery began to unfold, FEMA's rate of spending slowed. One month after passage, roughly two-thirds of the funds Congress had provided for disaster relief in the wake of the storm had yet to be allocated to hurricane relief work.[24]

Congress began to reallocate the unspent dollars from the DRF to other disaster assistance programs, first to the Community Disaster Loan Program,[25] and then more broadly. The Administration requested a $17.1 billion reallocation from the DRF to shore up non-FEMA disaster assistance programs in October 2005, but in December 2005 Congress approved a larger reallocation package included with the FY2006 Defense Appropriations Act that drew $23.4 billion from previously appropriated DRF monies and distributed them to several other agencies with storm-response needs.

The Congressional response to Hurricane Katrina was atypical in terms of the speed of its passage and amount of funding involved. Congress passed the largest non-war supplemental to date in support of the relief efforts before the scope of the needs had been fully assessed. It is not surprising, then, that the initial allocation would be reformulated to meet the emerging challenges of the recovery. The redistribution of DRF resources to disaster assistance in later legislation is, as was the case with P.L. 104-134, an example of disaster relief being *used as* an offset, rather than being *paid for by* an offset.

---

[21] H.Rept. 104-537, p. 560.

[22] The speed at which P.L. 109-61 and P.L. 109-62 were passed has few parallels. Even legislation drafted in response to the terrorist attacks of September 11, 2001, took seven days to be passed.

[23] Kathleen Pender, "The True Cost of Katrina," *San Francisco Chronicle*, September 27, 2005, p. D1.

[24] 2005 CQ Almanac, p.2-59

[25] $750 million was reallocated under P.L. 109-88 (119 Stat. 2061).

Offsets in the 112th Congress

First Session

In 2011, the House Appropriations Committee adopted an amendment that included an offset for a billion dollars of additional DRF funding added to the Homeland Security appropriations bill. This offset was unusual in that it drew funding from the Department of Energy rather than the Department of Homeland Security[26]—traditionally, offsets approved by the appropriations committees in the context of an annual appropriations bill have come from within the originating subcommittee's jurisdiction.

This offset was debated on the House Floor during consideration of the H.R. 2017,[27] and again during debate on a continuing resolution intended to provide stopgap funding for government operations and to replenish the DRF, which came historically close to depletion at the end of FY2011.[28]

Ultimately, an agreement was reached in September 2011 on a continuing resolution that paid for continued government operations and funded the DRF at an annualized rate of $2.65 billion, but without a supplemental appropriation for FY2011 or an offset.[29]

In the months before Congress addressed the continuing resolution, however, it passed the Budget Control Act (BCA, P.L. 112-25). Signed into law on August 2, 2011, this legislation provided a legislative context for the appropriations work for the coming fiscal decade. In addition to setting discretionary spending caps and a means to enforce them, the BCA included provisions to allow the caps to be adjusted upward to make budgetary room for disaster assistance and emergencies. The bill passed the House by a vote of 269-161 and the Senate by a vote of 74-26. The bill came one Democratic vote short in the House of having support of the majority of both caucuses of both the House and Senate. Despite this relatively broad support, discussions concerning the spending caps and budget mechanisms established by the BCA—including the cap adjustment provisions for disasters—continued into the debates on wrapping up the FY2012 appropriations legislation.

Toward the end of December 2011, the House of Representatives took up three pieces of legislation under a single rule for debate: a consolidated appropriations act (H.R. 2055, P.L. 112-74), a disaster assistance supplemental (H.R. 3672, P.L. 112-77), and an offset package (H.Con.Res. 94). P.L. 112-74 provided $700 million for the DRF, P.L. 112-77 provided an additional $8.1 billion in disaster assistance (including $6.4 billion for the DRF), and the offset package would have provided a 1.83% across-the-board rescission to pay for the additional disaster assistance. While all three pieces of legislation passed the House, the Senate only passed

---

[26] Title VI, H.R. 2017 (as Reported in the House).

[27] "Department of Homeland Security Appropriations Act, 2012," House debate, *Congressional Record*, vol. 157, part 1 (June 1, 2011), pp. H3832-H3835.

[28] "Continuing Appropriations Act, 2012," House debate, *Congressional Record*, vol. 157, part 1 (September 22, 2011), pp. H6389-H6410.

[29] P.L. 112-33 (125 Stat. 366).

---

the consolidated appropriations act and supplemental, rejecting the offset package by a vote of 43-56.[30]

Chairman Harold Rogers of the House Appropriations Committee clearly stated the purpose of H.Con.Res. 94 was to offset the $8.1 billion in additional disaster assistance.[31] Ranking Member Norman Dicks indicated immediately thereafter that the minority opinion was that the resolution was unnecessary, but did not object to its provisions.[32] The Senate did not address the resolution directly in floor debate, although several Senators noted that the disaster supplemental was within the flexibility provided under the BCA.[33]

Ultimately, despite this legislative activity, the first session of the 112th Congress ended without offsets being applied to supplemental appropriations for the DRF.

Hurricane Sandy

On October 29, 2012, shortly after the beginning of FY2013, Hurricane Sandy made landfall in New Jersey.[34] According to wire service reports a month afterwards, the storm killed at least 125 people in the United States and had $62 billion in damage attributed to it.[35] In late November and early December 2012, official estimates of the damage began to become public, and calls came from affected delegations for a supplemental appropriations package to provide assistance.[36] Toward the end of November 2012, Senator Saxby Chambliss indicated that he expected disaster assistance to be offset,[37] and House Majority Leader Eric Cantor indicated that disaster assistance should stay within the limits outlined by the BCA.[38] The White House has not yet released a request for a supplemental to fund Hurricane Sandy recovery, so it is not clear whether the allowable adjustment for disaster assistance for FY2013 will cover the additional resources sought for this fiscal year.

---

[30] U.S. Congress, House Committee on Appropriations, *Summary: Fiscal Year 2012 FInal Consolidated Appropriations Bill*, 112th Cong., 1st sess., December 15, 2011.

[31] Rep. Harold Rogers, "Correcting the Enrollment of H.R. 3672," House debate, *Congressional Record*, vol. 157, part 1 (December 16, 2011), p. H9903.

[32] Rep. Norman Dicks, "Correcting the Enrollment of H.R. 3672," House debate, *Congressional Record*, vol. 157, part 1 (December 16, 2011), p. H9903.

[33] "Military Construction and Veterans Affairs and Related Agencies Appropriations Act, 2012—Conference Report," and "Correcting the Enrollment of H.R. 3672," remarks in the Senate, *Congressional Record*, vol. 157, part 1 (December 17, 2011), pp. S8753-8759.

[34] While "Sandy" evolved from a tropical storm to a hurricane to a "post-tropical cyclone," for simplicity, this report applies the term "hurricane" to any storm that was at one point designated by the National Weather Service as a hurricane. For information on Sandy's official designation as it came ashore, see "Hurricane Sandy's Transition to a Post-Tropical Cyclone," available at http://www.nhc.noaa.gov/news/20121027_pa_sandyTransition.pdf.

[35] Associated Press, "What We Know About Superstorm Sandy a Month Later," November 29, 2012. Available at http://bigstory.ap.org/article/what-we-know-about-superstorm-sandy-month-later.

[36] Koss, Geof, "Senate Democrats Preparing Disaster Response Bills" CQ News, November 14, 2012. Available at http://www.cq.com/doc/news-4175335.

[37] Young, Kerry and Niels Lesniewski, "Republicans Say they Expect Spending Offsets for Sandy Disaster Aid," CQ News, November 29, 2012. Available at http://www.cq.com/doc/news-4181820?wr= bzR2QWhQbmtjMGxjdG52NXplMSo0UQ.

[38] "Disaster Relief Package Should Stay Within Spending Limits, Cantor Says," CQ News, November 30, 2012. Available at http://www.cq.com/doc/news-4183092?wr=bzR2QWhQbmtjMGtjTThKQWl2TERpQQ.

Considerations for Congress

As Congress resolves the FY2013 budget, and deals with requests for supplemental funding for disaster relief and recovery for Hurricane Sandy and other catastrophes, it will have to determine how to handle requests for disaster assistance, which, in all likelihood, will exceed the allowable adjustment for disaster relief under the Budget Control Act.[39]

Should supplemental disaster assistance be offset?

With the one exception noted above (P.L. 104-19), Congress has not fully offset supplemental funding for the DRF since 1990, although it has provided some offsets at times for disaster assistance. However, the appropriations process for FY2012 saw extensive debate on this topic over the course of the year as the level of funding available in the DRF declined. While the immediate risk of depleting the DRF at the end of FY2011 has been resolved, funding the federal response to Hurricane Sandy in the near and long term and its implications for the BCA structure will likely keep this issue under active discussion.

Traditionally, supplemental appropriations for disaster assistance, including the DRF, are requested after the disaster has struck and are on the scale of hundreds of millions to billions of dollars. Although initial emergency needs have usually been met before Congress provides funding, Congress generally faces political pressure to respond in a timely fashion to ensure needed relief resources are available beyond the immediate term. Adding the additional step to the process of identifying offsets would extend the time it takes for Congress to respond.

The most common types of offsets are spending cuts. At best, it would be difficult in a time of crisis to identify single sources of cuts in the discretionary budget that could be used to offset hundreds of millions of dollars of requested spending in response to a major disaster. Across-the-board cuts would be another means of offsetting these costs. Although they can be relatively simple to calculate and execute, it is possible that unintended consequences could result, potentially cutting programs important to the recovery of the area affected by the disaster.

Offsets could also be made through raising additional revenues to cover costs from the disaster. However, raising revenues carries political implications for some members of Congress, and there are significant obstacles in both the House and Senate to a combined revenue and appropriations bill. The House Ways and Means and Senate Finance committees are the committees of jurisdiction for revenue matters, while the House and Senate Appropriations committees have jurisdiction over discretionary spending of that revenue. The regular procedures of the House and Senate provide for separate consideration of revenue and appropriations legislation. Rule XXI in the House mandates that legislative provisions are barred from general appropriations bills. Most revenue raising provisions would qualify as legislative and therefore would not be in order. The Senate's Rule XVI serves a similar purpose. In accordance with the Constitution, revenue provisions must begin in the House, further complicating any possible Senate effort to initiate the

---

[39] For a discussion of the Budget Control Act, see CRS Report R41965, *The Budget Control Act of 2011*, by Bill Heniff Jr., Elizabeth Rybicki, and Shannon M. Mahan. For a more detailed discussion of the allowable adjustment for disaster assistance, see CRS Report R42352, *An Examination of Federal Disaster Relief Under the Budget Control Act*, by Bruce R. Lindsay, William L. Painter, and Francis X. McCarthy.

use of such provisions as offsets. While House rules are waived periodically, the appearance of revenue provisions in appropriations bills is rare.

Based on the historical evidence presented, offsetting supplemental funding for the DRF would be a change in the standard practice of Congress. One of the first questions that then arises is whether or not the current situation warrants a change to this traditional pattern of action. The primary focus of the discussion thus far has been the relative severity of the present budgetary situation—Congress may consider how much our current practice of funding disaster needs contribute to the deficit and debt. One complicating factor in assessing this is the inherent unpredictability of disasters. Identifying emerging trends in events that cannot be accurately forecast in terms of timing, frequency, or magnitude and then determining if those trends warrant policy change is extremely difficult, especially with such high-impact events as disasters in regards to human, economic, and political costs.

There is also a question of fairness—making a change to the way disaster assistance is approached by Congress may disadvantage those hit by disasters in the future compared to those hit by disasters in the past, either by adding constraints on the amount of aid provided or by incurring delays in the process due to the processes needed to identify and secure offsets. On the other hand, the government constantly changes policies and practices to save money and to improve efficiency, changing the availability or timing of assistance through a variety of other programs. While some may benefit or suffer as a result, that is in many cases not adequate justification in itself for not attempting to make needed reforms.

As noted above, one potential impact of requiring a search for offsets in the immediate wake of a disaster is that it might delay the availability of federal relief funds. Opponents of offsets note that developing options to pay for disaster assistance may slow the delivery of that aid, especially as recent budget reductions have arguably thinned the availability of quickly agreeable offsets. Also, the urgency of the process may not permit the necessary careful review of programs facing sudden reductions. Proponents might well argue that given the initial failures to deliver aid in the wake of Hurricane Katrina, an accelerated timeline for Congressional action does not, on its own, beget an effective, efficient response.

Should disaster assistance be funded through emergency designations?

The BCA provides statutory definitions that, depending how Congress applies them, could change congressional precedent for handling disaster assistance.

Emergency designations have been used in the past to provide additional funding without violating caps on discretionary budget authority established by Congressional budget resolutions. Most supplemental disaster assistance in the past has been designated as emergency funding. One of the primary reasons that supplemental funding for the DRF had not been offset over the period of analysis used in this report is the simple fact that it hasn't had to be offset, given the availability of the emergency funding mechanism to work around the budget caps.

Disaster relief is defined under the BCA as assistance provided pursuant to the declaration of a major disaster under the Stafford Act.[40] This definition is made as part of creating an "allowable adjustment" to the discretionary budget caps for disaster relief. The BCA also says that "Appropriations considered disaster relief under this subparagraph in a fiscal year shall not be eligible" for the unlimited adjustment available for emergencies.[41]

Taking a broad reading of these provisions, one could see a future where disaster relief funding would be constrained by the size of the allowable adjustment (possibly in a year with multiple costly disasters), and that the option of providing emergency funding for major disasters would no longer be on the table. However, the law makes no such explicit delineation—despite the creation of two adjustment mechanisms for emergencies and for disaster relief, there is no positive statement that stated that the emergency funding adjustment may not be used to pay for disaster assistance or relief. Additionally, it is worth noting that initially, no enforcement mechanisms were provided in the BCA to prevent broad application of disaster relief or emergency designations.[42]

Congress could choose to constrain itself from going beyond the allowable adjustment, requiring offsets for further disaster relief from the regular budget, or—in a more proactive step—simply funding a larger proportion of disaster relief in the base budget to begin with. The appropriate level of base funding for the DRF has been a recurring issue over the last fifteen years.[43] On the other hand, in the absence of an explicit prohibition on the practice as noted above, Congress could also use emergency designations to fund disaster relief in excess of the allowable adjustment under the BCA.

In the current budgetary environment, using allowable adjustments or emergency designations results in deficit spending. Strictly conforming to the budget limits means that meeting unexpected demands for resources (such as for disaster relief) will likely result in unplanned reductions in other parts of the budget, reducing services available through other programs.

However, the consequences of a political backlash from overuse of emergency authorities should not be ignored. Overly broad use of emergency or disaster relief designations to cover spending not appropriate to those categories could lead to more strictly drafted budget control legislation in the future, reducing or eliminating flexibility that may otherwise be needed on short notice in dire circumstances.

---

[40] Sec. 102, P.L. 112-25.

[41] Sec. 101, P.L. 112-25.

[42] The original BCA removed the Senate's point of order against overly broad use of the emergency designation. The point of order was restored by the Temporary Payroll Tax Cut Continuation Act of 2011 (P.L. 112-78).

[43] An "emergency fund" proposed in 1998 was meant to provide a cushion for the DRF and reduce the need for supplementals. Congress disagreed with the proposal, but did increase the base budget amount from that point forward.

Appendix. Historical Data

To show the relative impact of offsets on supplemental spending and the DRF, **Table 1** provides a breakdown of all appropriations bills that have become law carrying both supplemental spending and rescissions since 1990. The columns indicate the total amount of supplemental appropriations in the bill, the rescissions in the bill, and the amount of additional funding for the DRF. The table then notes whether there are provisions indicating that the funding for the DRF is offset. The table also notes when DRF funding has been used as an offset for other activities.

Table A-1. Bills with Supplemental Appropriations and Rescissions 1990-2012

(In millions of dollars)

Year / Bill number	P.L.	Informal Title	Date Enacted	Supplemental Appropriation	Rescission	Disaster Relief Fund (DRF)	Linkage	Notes
2012		No supplemental appropriations with rescission were enacted for FY2012.						
2011		No supplemental appropriations were enacted for FY2011.						
2010								
H.R. 4899	111-212	Supplemental Appropriations Act of 2010	7/29/2010	42,417	305	5,100	None	
H.R. 5874	111-224	U.S. Patent and Trademark Office Supplemental Appropriations Act, 2010	8/10/2010	129	129	0	n/a	
H.R. 6080	111-230	Making Emergency Supplemental Appropriations for Border Security for 2010	8/13/2010	600	100	0	n/a	
2009								
H.R. 2346	111-32	Supplemental Appropriations Act, 2009	6/24/2009	111,605	5,754	(20)	n/a	The bill rescinded $20 million from the DRF.
2008								
H.R. 2642	110-252	Supplemental Appropriations Act, 2008	6/30/2008	116,093	285	897	None	
H.R. 2638	110-329	Disaster Relief and Recovery Supplemental Appropriations Act, 2008	9/30/2008	22,879	20	7,960[a]	None	
2007								
H.R. 2206	110-28	Supplemental Appropriations Act for Defense, International Affairs, Other Security-Related Needs, and Hurricane Katrina Recovery, 2007	5/25/2007	120,918	939	4,110	None	
2006								

Offsets, Supplemental Appropriations, and the Disaster Relief Fund: FY1990–FY2013

Year / Bill number	P.L.	Informal Title	Date Enacted	Supplemental Appropriation	Rescission	Disaster Relief Fund (DRF)	Linkage	Notes
H.R. 2863	109-148	Division B of 2006 Defense Appropriations Act	12/30/2005	32,561	33,558	(23,409)	None, but the bill was fully offset	Rescinded $23,409 million from the DRF, plus a 1% across-the-board rescission. The bill was scored as a $997 million reduction in budget authority.
H.R. 4939	109-234	Emergency Supplemental Appropriations Act for Defense, the Global War on Terror, and Hurricane Recovery, 2006	6/15/2006	95,695	1,265	6,000	None	
2005								
H.R. 1268	109-13	Emergency Supplemental Appropriations Act for Defense, the Global War on Terror, and Tsunami Relief, 2005	5/11/2005	83,555	1,473	0	n/a	
2004								
H.R. 3829	108-106	Supplemental for Defense / Iraq / Afghanistan	11/6/2003	87,583	3	500	None	
H.R. 4613	108-287	Defense Appropriations Act, 2005 (Titles VIII, IX, and X)	8/5/2004	28,256	100	0	None	
2003								
H.R. 1559	108-11	Emergency Wartime Supplemental Appropriations Act, 2003	4/16/2003	79,193	3	0	n/a	
2002								
H.R. 4775	107-206	Emergency Supplemental and Rescissions, 2002	8/2/2002	26,554	2,337	0	n/a	
2001								
H.R. 2216	107-20	Emergency Supplemental and Rescissions, 2001	7/24/2001	8,979	2,436	0	n/a	
2000								
H.R. 4425	106-246	Military Construction, 2001	7/13/2000	15,608	470	0	n/a	
1999								
H.R. 1664	106-51	Emergency Steel and Emergency Oil and Gas Guaranteed Loan Act, 1999	8/17/1999	270	270	0	n/a	

Year / Bill number	P.L.	Informal Title	Date Enacted	Supplemental Appropriation	Rescission	Disaster Relief Fund (DRF)	Linkage	Notes
H.R. 1141	106-31	Emergency Supplemental Appropriations and Rescissions, 1999	5/21/1999	13,097	1,749	900	None	
1998								
H.R. 3579	105-174	Emergency Supplemental Appropriations and Rescissions, 1998	5/1/1998	6,006	2,726	2,000	None	
1997								
H.R. 1871	105-18	1997 Supplemental for Disasters and Peacekeeping Efforts in Bosnia	6/12/1997	9,163	7,980	3,300	n/a	The DRF funding was contingent on a request from the Administration.
1996								
H.R. 3019	104-134	Omnibus Consolidated Appropriations and Rescissions Act, 1996	4/26/1996	555	2,644	222	None, but the bill was fully offset	The legislation was scored as a $2,089 million reduction in budget authority—$1,000 million of which was rescinded from the DRF.
H.R. 3610	104-208	Omnibus Consolidated Appropriations Act, 1997	9/30/1996	123	127	0	n/a	The legislation was scored as a $4 million reduction in budget authority.
1995								
H.R. 889	104-6	1995 Emergency Supplemental and Rescissions for Defense Readiness	4/10/1995	2,318	3,331	0	n/a	The legislation was scored as a $1,013 million reduction in budget authority.
H.R. 1944	104-19	1995 Emergency Supplemental and Rescissions for Antiterrorism and Oklahoma City Disaster	7/27/1995	7,453	15,992	6,550b	None, but the bill was fully offset	The legislation was scored as a $8,539 million reduction in budget authority.

Offsets, Supplemental Appropriations, and the Disaster Relief Fund: FY1990-FY2013

Year / Bill number	P.L.	Informal Title	Date Enacted	Supplemental Appropriation	Rescission	Disaster Relief Fund (DRF)	Linkage	Notes
1994								
H.R. 3759	103-211	1994 Emergency Supplemental (Los Angeles earthquake)	2/12/94	11,535	3,157	4,709	None	
1993								
H.R. 4624	103-327	1995 VA-HUD Appropriations	9/28/94	357	2	13	None	
H.R. 2118	103-50	1993 Spring Supplemental	7/2/1993	3,499	2,499	0	n/a	
1992								
H.R. 5132	102-302	1992 Emergency Disaster Assistance for Los Angeles and Chicago	6/22/92	1,191	8	300	None	
H.R. 5620	102-368	1992 Supplemental (Hurricanes Andrew, Iniki, Omar)	9/23/92	12,775	265	2,908	None	
1991								
H.R. 1281	102-27	Dire Emergency Supplemental Appropriations, 1991	4/10/91	5,255	323	0	n/a	
H.R. 2251	102-55	1991 Dire Emergency Supplemental for Iraqi Refugees	6/13/91	581	8	0	n/a	
1990								
H.R. 404	101-302	Dire Emergency Supplemental Appropriations, 1990	5/25/90	4,336	2,045	50	None	
1989								
H.R. 2402	101-45		6/30/1989	3,564				

Source: CRS analysis of CBO data and base legislation.

Notes:

a. $98 million of the $7,960 million for the DRF was transferred to the Disaster Assistance Direct Loan Program Account.

b. $3,275 million of the total for the DRF was contingent on a request for emergency funding from the administration.

Author Contact Information

William L. Painter
Analyst in Emergency Management and Homeland
Security Policy
wpainter@crs.loc.gov, 7-3335